Bloody Mary for the AERA Attendee's Soul

Bloody Mary for the AERA Attendee's Soul

Daniel H. Robinson
The University of Texas at Arlington

INFORMATION AGE PUBLISHING, INC.
Charlotte, NC • www.infoagepub.com

Library of Congress Cataloging-in-Publication Data

CIP record for this book is available from the Library of Congress
http://www.loc.gov

ISBNs: 978-1-64802-917-2 (Paperback)

978-1-64802-918-9 (Hardcover)

978-1-64802-919-6 (ebook)

CONTENTS

1. How to Save Money on Food...*1*

2. My Path to Grad School *5*

3. What Is AERA Anyway? *9*

4. From Kiewra to Kulhavy...*13*

5. How to Save Money on Beverages...*17*

6. The Awakening *21*

7. How to Save Money on Lodging...*25*

8. My First AERA—Boston, 1990 ....*27*

9. How to Save Money on Travel...*31*

10. Nebraska Act II *33*

11. How to Save Money at the Exhibits *37*

12. Mississippi State *39*

13. Working With Grad Students...*41*

14. South Dakota...*45*

15. Where to Publish? *49*

16. Louisville and Texas *53*

17. Recruiting Grad Students *57*

18. The Five-Tool Faculty Member *59*

19. Ranting About the Field of Education *63*

20. Reviewing and Editing *65*

References *69*

Figures *71*

About the Author *75*

CHAPTER 1

HOW TO SAVE MONEY ON FOOD

Chapters 1, 5, 7, 9, and 11 are intended for those who do not have a bottomless spending account and/or simply do not enjoy wasting money. The AERA conference is an expensive venture. And it gets more expensive every year. It is held in a large city and the prices for everything can be sticker shocking. In the good old days (early 90s for me), grad students could register for the conference for about $25. You could share a hotel room, book a flight, and your total bill for five days might be under $500. Today, the five-day experience can easily cost over $2,000. Grad students may not have much extra cash to begin with and junior faculty are likely only getting meager per diem reimbursements. So why not save some money if you can?

Here's how to spend less money on meals and also not waste your time during the meal. First and foremost, do not, I repeat, DO NOT accept an invitation to join a large group of people for dinner. I know it's flattering (so-and-so will be there!), sounds fun, and many of you have a hard time saying no. But this has nightmare written all over it. The dinner idea is usually the brainchild of someone who has lived in the host city and has a favorite restaurant that is sure to please everyone. This restaurant is going to be on the more expensive side. Once you have unwittingly accepted the invitation, here's how your evening will likely go.

Bloody Mary for the AERA Attendee's Soul, pp. 1–3
Copyright © 2022 by Information Age Publishing
www.infoagepub.com

Everyone will agree to meet in the lobby of one of the major conference hotels around 6 p.m. so you can all hop into cabs or Uber and go to the restaurant. Because eight people are going (eight?!!, yes, we try to be inclusive these days and the more, the merrier), the statistical chance that all eight will be in the lobby and ready to go at the designated time approaches and slams into zero. You will then spend the next 30 minutes calling, texting, and waiting for everyone to appear. Then you will wait another 15–20 minutes waiting on the transportation because you and everyone else who has not yet read this book will be trying to get a rideshare at the same time. When you finally arrive at the restaurant around 7 P.M. or later, you will learn that there is a 90-minute wait. Your 6:30 reservation is long past thanks to the person who was late arriving to the hotel lobby. Please continue to glare at that person throughout the evening. Then you will all huddle up, call an audible, and choose another restaurant where you can spend even more money on a rideshare only to find that they have a similar wait time. Even if you have reservations, when you finally get seated, wait forever to get your food, and enjoy your large group dinner, where you can really only talk with the people sitting adjacent to you because it is so loud, you can rest assured you will finish and get back to your hotel room after 10 P.M.—long after the receptions have ended. Congratulations, you have succeeded in wasting the entire evening so that you can chat with a few people. I hope they were the important ones. What's worse, you will likely spend between $50 and $100 on the meal. What's much worse, you have missed the receptions that ran from 7–9 P.M. Shame on you, amateur. Or worse, perhaps you and your friends are Walter Sobchak's kind of amateurs.

I recommend spending the following amount on evening meals: $0. Each night of the conference, there will be several receptions hosted by various universities and vendors (for-profit companies that come to AERA to woo clients). Over 90% of these receptions are open to conference attendees (they will say "invitation-only" otherwise). That means you can just show up and not feel guilty about not being invited or having some connection to the group that is hosting. There is FREE food. Sure, it's not going to be the same as your $100 meal at a fancy restaurant, but there is good food to be had if you find the right receptions. The vendor receptions (AIR, ETS, Westat, Pearson, etc.) have one purpose when they spend money on a reception—to impress existing and potential new clients. They WILL have good food. So, eat up when they begin around 7 P.M. You'll save a ton of money and chances are, if you hit enough receptions, you will get to meet a lot more people who are important to your career success than the inbred cronies that are all "legend in his own mind" Professor X's former students.

What about breakfast? Well, if you are doing the evening receptions correctly, you should be in no condition when you wake up to be craving breakfast. Instead, you should be dehydrated, ready for water and an anti-inflammatory pill, and go back to bed until 10 or 11 A.M. With a little more sleep and perhaps walking around the exhibits, you will need no more than a Dr. Pepper to make it to lunchtime. If you are one of those annoying people who gets up early, feels great, works out, and so forth, then find a bagel place where you can get breakfast for less than $10. Don't go to a restaurant in the hotel. Your bill will be over $30.

Lunch is really the only meal where you should ever have to spend your own money. Don't eat anywhere near the major hotels or convention center. Those places are overpriced and usually crappy. Do your homework. Scout out the decent, cheaper delicatessens and diners a few blocks away where you can get something good. For example, if you are in Philadelphia, go find a good Philly Cheesesteak joint. If you are in San Francisco, take a walk or the trolley to Fisherman's Wharf and get a bread bowl filled with clam chowder. If you are in New Orleans, get a muffuletta or some seafood in the French Quarter. The point is, make the lunch count. It's the only time you should be spending money. Better yet, if you need to meet with a book publisher, schedule the meeting over lunch. They will be happy to pick up the tab.

If you take a significant other with you to AERA, the above advice is off the table. The non-academic, significant other may insist on dining at more expensive venues. That's your fault. If you follow my advice, no self-respecting, nonacademic person should ever want to attend AERA again after the first conference. As one of my mentors once replied when I asked if his significant other would be attending the upcoming conference, "Dan, that's like bringing shampoo to a hotel." AERA is not a date vacation. It is also not great for kids. Of course, I understand if your situation prevents you from going alone. But you have been warned. It is really impossible to both "do" AERA appropriately to enhance your career and also bring along someone who simply wants to enjoy a vacation with you. Attempt to do both at your own peril. But my advice is to leave them at home and take them on a better vacation at another time when you can devote 100% of yourself to just them.

CHAPTER 2

MY PATH TO GRAD SCHOOL

Chapters 2, 4, 6, 8, 10, 12, and 14 tell the story of my academic journey until 2000. Similar to the purpose of the other advice chapters, my hope is that you will learn something to help you in your academic journey by sharing mine.

My story begins in the small town (pop. about 1,100 now, maybe 400 when I was born) of Lawton, Iowa—located just east of Sioux City. There's something peculiar about the northwestern part of Iowa in that several AERA-type folks grew up there. Paul Nichols, who worked at ACT and Wisconsin-Milwaukee, also grew up in Lawton. Mark Grabe (since retired from the University of North Dakota) is from the small town of Kingsley, about 15 miles away, and Sarah Peterson (University of Texas at El Paso) is from Paullina, another 50 miles or so to the north. Even Marlene Schommer (retired from Wichita State University), Marlynn Griffin (Georgia Southern University), and I'm sure a few others (Camilo Guerrero) in educational psychology spent at least part of their youth in Iowa. Go figure.

My family was working class. My dad was a bridge construction foreman and my mom was a billing clerk for the local phone company. My older brother is recently retired and worked for that same phone company for over 20 years. I guess like most places, a majority of the people who are raised there end up spending the rest of their lives near Lawton, Iowa. I should have been one of them. I was a B student in high school, your garden-variety slacker, never realizing my academic potential as I was much too concerned with goofing off and getting a laugh or two. Come to think

---

of it, those of you who know me probably think, based on my AERA conference behavior and priorities, that I have not changed a bit. You would be correct.

I graduated in 1983, one month after my mother succumbed to a six-month battle with non-Hodgkins lymphoma. For added effect, her funeral was the day before my senior prom. I had completed my application to the University of Nebraska in her hospital room and that fall I was enrolled in the teacher education program, secondary education, social sciences. The truth is I had no idea what I wanted to do. I wanted to attend college because I knew it would be fun and I would get to drink often. My mother had attended college for two years and received an associate degree. She pushed my brother and I to attend college to have a better life. I chose teaching as a major because it seemed like the teachers I had in high school had a pretty easy life with summers off. There was absolutely no passion for the career. I chose Nebraska because my brother was there, and I wanted to go to the football games. My brother, who was and remains much smarter than me, struggled in the engineering program, eventually dropping out, so I was determined to not take the same path. History was a subject I liked, and I thought I would stand a fighting chance of not failing if I took easy courses. I was pathetic, but right.

After five years, with one year off, including a semester at Iowa State and another semester working fulltime at Kmart (boy, did that make me appreciate college!), to avoid out of state tuition fees until I could get my residency in Nebraska, I graduated with a respectable GPA, armed and dangerous to go out and be a poor excuse for a teacher in the public schools. Luckily for me and for all those students, I realized how lousy I was right before I graduated and had the good sense to do whatever I could to avoid the real world. I had made a poor choice in terms of my vocation (absent any passion for it) and there was only one way to avoid teaching without appearing to be a loser to my family and friends. I would go to graduate school. Grad school is the perfect place for those who don't want to work and still want to drink irresponsibly without having the guilt of being unemployed. The logic behind my choice of what to pursue and at what school was as ridiculous as my previous choice of wanting to be a high school history teacher. I knew a professor in curriculum and instruction (C&I) at Nebraska, the late Keith Prichard, who advised me to avoid C&I and instead go into educational psychology where he thought the market was much better. I could pursue a master's degree that would still allow me to teach high school but would also permit me to explore nonteaching options, whatever those were. I gladly took his advice and sent applications to Arizona State, Texas, and, of course, Nebraska (in case ASU and Texas wouldn't take me). ASU and Texas were located in the Sun Belt and having spent all my life in the Midwest, I was interested in seeing some different scenery where I could ride my motorcycle year-round.

Based on my decent GPA and GRE scores, I was accepted to all three programs. I was pushed by Prichard to go to Texas as it had the best academic reputation of the three. I spoke with Guy Manaster, who was department chair of educational psychology at the time and asked him for a half-time (20-hour) assistantship. I was not going to move to Austin with no job prospects. Remember, this was 1988 when even minimum wage jobs were hard to find. Guy told me he would try his best and a week later he informed me that he could not find an assistantship. I later learned that this was the norm in Texas. First year students did not get assistantships—you have to wait until your second year, which makes recruiting difficult. I thanked Guy Manaster and said good-bye to Texas. Years later when Guy became my colleague, I discovered that he was even nicer in person. And he gave me great advice that a young faculty member needed.

Next, I contacted Arizona State and Gerald Helmstadter, the department chair. ASU did better, but not good enough. Helmstadter offered me a 10-hour assistantship, which was equivalent to about $260 a month. That would barely cover my rent. I had a cousin who lived in Tempe, and she offered to let me room with her for $250 per month. I asked Helmstadter for a 20-hour assistantship, thinking I would also have to eat, but was told there was no way that was going to happen in the fall of 1988. I told him that I would enroll at Nebraska and check with him again in late November for the Spring Semester. Nebraska was my default plan as I could continue to work as a resident assistant in the dorms. The job was not glamorous, but it was free room and board. During the summers, I could live with my dad and work (on a survey crew—up to 70 hours a week) to pay for my tuition and other expenses during the school year. This was the only option I could afford. My parents hadn't created a college fund nor did my dad have any other extra cash for me. If I wanted a college degree, I had to figure out how to pay for it. To this day I have never resented that my dad did not pay my way. Instead, I feel that the value I place on my education is greater due to the fact that I paid for it.

CHAPTER 3

WHAT IS AERA ANYWAY?

Fast forward a bit to the spring of 1989 when I was a grad student at Arizona State University. I was taking a theories of learning course from Ray Kulhavy—definitely a guy who knew how to "do" AERA the right way! The course was outstanding and ultimately caused me to change my focus from human development to cognition and learning. Because I had an assistantship, I was fortunate to have an office in the same suite as Kulhavy. This allowed me to have a few conversations outside of class and I ended up, sort of, on his research crew. One day he asked me if I was going to AERA. I had no idea what AERA was. He proceeded to explain that it was an annual conference that was the largest international gathering of educational researchers. This was simply the place to be if you were a player or wanted to be a player one day. It was being held in San Francisco that year. I told him that I hadn't submitted anything and thus was not presenting. He said that wouldn't be a problem, and in fact, the best way to attend AERA for the first time is to go as a nonpresenter. I thanked him and told him I would try my best.

Grad school in 1989 for me was a bit different than it is today for most students I know. I was getting a nine-month, 20-hour per week assistantship that paid $520 per month. My rent was $250 without utilities. That left very little for other necessary expenses— books, food, happy hours, and so forth. After assessing my financial situation, I determined that I would not be able to afford the flight from Phoenix to San Francisco, plus lodging, registration, and so forth. I informed Kulhavy of my decision the

Bloody Mary for the AERA Attendee's Soul, pp. 9–11
Copyright © 2022 by Information Age Publishing
www.infoagepub.com

next time I saw him and also thanked him for the opportunity. I told him I would definitely submit something and attend next year. I still remember his expression to this day. He looked at me as if I cared nothing about my field, scholarship, networking, and so forth. That one hurt. But there was nothing I could do short of taking out a loan. I mean, I was dirt poor as a grad student.

Kulhavy was right. Attending AERA is important if you have any plans to be an academic one day. As much as I have a sort of love-hate relationship with the organization and the conference, I have always strongly encouraged my grad students to attend—even if they are not presenting. And yes, it is preferable to attend without the stress of presenting for your first time. That way you can fully absorb and experience the conference. Your first AERA conference will be eye-opening. Lots of people, lots of name badges, all scurrying to sessions. The sessions themselves are strange. Poster sessions aren't so bad because if you are lost and clueless, like I usually am, you can blend in with others easily. Roundtables are weird. A bunch of tables in rooms with various numbers of people sitting at them ranging from zero (no one showed up, not even the paper presenter) to 20 (with only 12 available chairs). I remember seeing throngs of female grad students crowded around a roundtable where Chuck Perfetti was holding court years ago. I thought to myself if that is me in 20 years, I would consider myself successful. Well, I'm still waiting for all those students when I sit at my lonely table. And no, I'm not creepy.

Poster and roundtable sessions are weird in that even though you bring copies of your paper, a few strangers will always say, "tell me about your study." Do you start from the beginning and give them the 10-minute version? Do you take the rude approach, which I have been tempted to do more than once as I have sat there with a fierce hangover, and hand them your paper and tell them to read it? Honestly, posters and roundtables are great opportunities for you to hone your elevator speech (one-minute version of your paper) and also meet and network with new people. I remember being starstruck when someone like Patricia Alexander, Dick Anderson, Isabel Beck, David Berliner, Ann Brown, Lyn Corno, Joel Levin, Rich Mayer, Mike Pressley, or Howard Wainer stopped by to talk and check out my poster. That will happen to you, too. Just be ready. Pop in a breath mint. Have that Dr Pepper handy to cure the dry mouth.

The paper sessions are perhaps the worst part about AERA. You typically have four to six presenters each trying to cram over 30 minutes worth of slides into their 10 minutes of allotted time. The session chair usually does a terrible job of corralling such overprepared speakers and the result is the session runs late. The poor discussant, who was promised 15 minutes at the end, usually has zero to five minutes instead. Few discussants actually do their job and provide true critiques. Most try to be nice and just praise the papers and presenters. You wonder why you spent one and a half to two hours sitting in a hot, cramped room to witness the absolute worst display of pedagogy from the world's best educators. This experience will motivate you to seek out the evening's receptions. That's good. This epiphany will direct you to the main purpose of AERA—networking.

CHAPTER 4

FROM KIEWRA TO KULHAVY

Back to the fall of 1988, I was enrolled in the development program (once again, the development choice was a shot in the dark) in the Department of Educational Psychology at Nebraska. I enrolled in three courses (a full load) and had even more free time than during my undergrad days (compared to five courses) for drinking and just goofing around. You see, like many clueless, meandering grad students, I was under the false impression that grad students just did coursework and didn't need to become involved in research. I simply thought that life was good and easily settled into my leisurely schedule. One of my courses was learning and cognition, taught by a brand-new assistant professor at the University of Nebraska, Ken Kiewra. Taking Ken's class would alter my career path. Ken got me interested in learning and cognition due to his extraordinary teaching style. He used demonstrations of actual experiments where the class served as the subjects and saw the phenomena first-hand. To this day, I shamelessly attempt to copy Ken's style when I teach similar courses. Although my area was development, I became intrigued with learning and how students could be more effective learners. Late that November I received a phone call from Helmstadter at ASU early one morning as I had a nasty hangover. He had found a 20-hour assistantship and wanted to know if I would come to Tempe in January. Without even thinking, I accepted. The call came when there was snow on the ground. As I spoke with him, looking out at the arctic tundra of Nebraska, I envisioned palm trees. My interest in ASU was completely nonacademic. I liked the photos of swimming pools in all their propaganda

Bloody Mary for the AERA Attendee's Soul, pp. 13–15
Copyright © 2022 by Information Age Publishing
www.infoagepub.com

materials. When I told Ken Kiewra that I was going to ASU, he said I should get in touch with a guy named Kulhavy.

On an early, chilly morning in January 1989, I said good-bye to my teary-eyed dad and plowed through a snowdrift to get out of our driveway with my 1978 Monte Carlo, pulling a trailer that carried my motorcycle. My only thoughts as I drove out of town were about getting to ride a motorcycle year-round in Arizona's warm weather. Again, not many academic thoughts, goals, dreams, etc. occupied my mind before 1989. I enrolled in three courses again, with one of them being a theories of learning course. On the first day of class, this distinguished-looking man entered the classroom and stared at each student. He introduced himself as Dr. Kulhavy and proceeded to tell us how to succeed in his class. We were encouraged to bring cassette tape recorders as he lectured quite fast. He also told us that he didn't want to be interrupted with questions during the lectures. We should write down our questions and ask him after class was over. I remember Kulhavy would be lecturing and at the 45-minute mark, about 20 tape recorders would all stop in unison. He would pause while we scrambled to the front table to eject our tapes, flip them over and hit the record button. After each class I would go back to my office and play the tape to fill in the missing information in my notes. About two hours of lecture followed by about three hours more.

Such a teaching style today would certainly result in several student complaints to the department chair. What kind of professor would have the audacity to teach in this way? There is only one kind. The kind of professor whose lectures are so entertaining that you quickly forget how silly you may look trying to keep up with him. Kulhavy had something called stage presence. Very few instructors have this and not many actors have it either. Clint Eastwood has the ability to make you focus on him even when other actors on the screen are speaking. Kulhavy had the ability to hold students' attention for well over an hour.

I've known only one other professor who could maintain such attention, but his style was different. He constantly interacted with students, asking them questions. I had the privilege of seeing the late John Glover in action at the University of Nebraska when I was an undergrad. I was taking an ed psych course from a grad student named Alice Corkill in the fall of 1986 when one day John Glover showed up to inform us that Alice had suffered a cycling accident and would be back next week. Glover proceeded to give one of the best interactive lectures I had ever seen. Completely without preparation. His energy level was similar to Kulhavy's. I regret not getting to know John Glover, the scholar, who died tragically in 1989 at age 40, ending an amazing career. And Alice Corkill, his student, went on to an academic career at UNLV, and remains a good friend.

Taking Kulhavy's class would alter my career path in the same way Kiewra's class had done. I was hooked on cognition and learning and decided it was time to bail out of the development program. I had sat in on a research meeting of some development faculty and grad students and came away fully convinced that if I continued my present course, I would never graduate. Lots of talking, posturing, and so forth, but no progress. In fact, one of my fellow development grad students at ASU who had started a few years before I arrived in 1989 was still ABD 10 years later! I shudder when I think back on how my life could have been so much different than it is now. Avoid the dementors!

CHAPTER 5

HOW TO SAVE MONEY ON BEVERAGES

Several years ago, I interviewed my friend, mentor, and occasional tennis partner Gene Glass, and it appeared in the *Educational Researcher* (Robinson, 2004). At the end of the interview, I slipped in a sentence that to this day is a source of pride for me, "AERA as an organization is in trouble. For Gene Glass, myself, and several others, the "R" now stands mostly for reunion, reconnecting, and receptions, rather than research" (p. 30). I'm proud because I was able to get in a shot at AERA—and it appeared in one of their own journals. One of the reviewers noticed it but I didn't change it. I love being naughty and getting away with it.

Notice that I suggested that the R in AERA could stand for receptions. Quite simply, I believe that the evening receptions at AERA are the most important part of the conference. If you "do" the receptions the right way you can save considerable money on adult beverages. Of course, this can only occur if you end up at an open bar reception.

Probably my saddest experiences at AERA, other than when I am foolish enough to attend a "research" paper session, are when I walk into an evening reception and discover that the bar is a cash bar rather than an open bar. If I may quote one of my favorite television characters—Frank Barone, "it is to be a full bar. Free of charge. With top-shelf hooch. Read your bible."

Now, I don't mind spending a couple of bucks on a beer. Those of you who know me, stop laughing and rolling your eyes. But when the reception is held at a hotel or convention center, the price of a domestic beer approaches $10. Ten dollars! Needless to say, if one has a limited budget for AERA expenses, cash bar receptions can eat up a budget quickly.

In the movie *Wedding Crashers* (Dobkin, 2005) John and Jeremy are planning their attack for that summer's wedding schedule.

"How many are cash bars?"

"Great question. I love where your head's at."

Unless you plan to wear a fake Purple Heart medal to get people to buy you drinks all night, you need my advice. I'd say about two thirds or more of evening receptions at AERA will have cash bars. To find the other third where you can drink for free, you need to be smart. *What I am about to tell you may ruin AERA from now on for me and my colleagues.* It's like a fishing guide giving up the location of the best spot. But this advice could very well help you cover the cost of this book in one evening.

What do you like better, Christmas or AERA reception week?

Remember what I said in the previous chapter about the vendor receptions being more likely to have better food than your typical university reception? Well, that also holds in terms of vendor receptions having a higher probability of open bars instead of cash bars. Vendors want your business, and they want attendees to have a positive experience at the reception. You don't get that if you gouge prospective clients for alcohol. So, *Rule #1: Scout out the vendor receptions.* The bar may not be fully open, but you can at least expect to get one or two drink tickets. Then you stick-and-move on to the next one. You may end up hitting more than five receptions in one evening. Or you may find the perfect setting with free food, drinks, and excellent company. If so, spend the full two hours there. Don't forget to grab two drinks before last call. Then you can continue to hang out in the room while the staff tear down and clean up and eventually ask you to leave for the third time. You can always stuff one of the longneck beers inside your blazer as you leave. THAT is why they put those pockets there, by the way.

Some university receptions can also have great food and free drinks. But remember that they play by different rules. Public universities can spend public funds to host a reception with free food. But when it comes to paying for alcohol, most need to use a different account with fewer restrictions. Some of the larger universities are able to do this, as are ones who simply have an education dean who effectively hides away donor money in a separate account. Others cannot. If you are wanting to attend some of these latter receptions so you might be able to meet some researchers in your area whose work you admire, just remember that there may be a cash bar there. Heck, like Chazz Reinhold, I will throw in a cash bar reception now and then. But open bars are to cash bars what funerals are to weddings. It's like fishing with dynamite. If it is very important for you to be there, be sure to use your one drink wisely and talk to that person you absolutely have to meet. Or better yet, sneak in a longneck from an open bar reception that you just left. Remember the pocket.

More probable, on average, to have open bar receptions are the larger private universities (e.g., Harvard, Stanford, Columbia, etc.). *Rule #2: After the vendor receptions, private universities come next in terms of priority, followed by the large public universities.* Private universities have fewer restrictions on their spending than the public ones. They can purchase alcohol. Finally, a team effort is usually required to find the open bar receptions. If you like to "reception hop" as I do, gather a few people, no more than three to four (remember my admonition about large groups going to dinner), where each person can scout the 7 P.M. receptions and quickly text the group concerning the open bar/cash bar situation. Then the others can quickly meet up before going to the next reception. *Rule #3: Divide and conquer.*

Before closing this chapter, let me say a bit about the purpose of AERA in general, receptions in particular, and drinking alcohol specifically. The purpose is NOT to simply find free drinks. If that is your sole motivation, then you are not doing anything to advance your career. Your purpose should be to meet and connect with important people with whom you might collaborate one day. AERA is for networking. If you do the evening receptions right, you can get much more face time with the people you seek than if you attend a bunch of daytime sessions. And the conversation is much easier at a reception than at a crowded session where little time exists for chatting. Remember, always keep your focus. Use the AERA conference experience to advance your career and have fun doing so. But don't overdrink to the point where you make an ass of yourself, jeopardize your career, and endanger your life or others. Holding your alcohol and acting appropriately is something you should take seriously. And continue to do it for the rest of your life.

CHAPTER 6

THE AWAKENING

In September 1989, I went to see Kulhavy to inquire about switching programs to learning and cognition. Kulhavy could see just how unfocused and clueless I really was. He proceeded to dress me down with a wake-up call about what it would take to realize my goal of becoming a professor in learning and cognition. I would need to get busy conducting research and presenting and publishing papers. I was shocked as I had thought that I didn't have to do any research until my dissertation. I have since discovered that many grad students are just as clueless as I was and make sure to give them the same wake-up call. To my chagrin, Kulhavy also told me that he was no longer taking on any new grad students and that if I wanted to work on research, I should see Bill Stock. Kulhavy was being courted by Florida State at this time and was convinced that he would be leaving ASU at the end of the year. He didn't want to leave any students hanging when he left. I then met with Stock, a statistics professor. I learned that he and Kulhavy were directing several research projects and that I would be given a chance to get involved if I would work hard and meet deadlines. I remember Stock telling me that the main goal of this effort was to "do good science." I didn't know what that meant back then but have come to understand it better over time.

Stock ordered me to check in with John Behrens, an advanced grad student on the team. John was a no-nonsense type of guy and gave me much needed straight talk, like Kulhavy and Stock had done. John was my unofficial mentor during my three semesters at ASU. He gave me more

Bloody Mary for the AERA Attendee's Soul, pp. 21–23
Copyright © 2022 by Information Age Publishing
www.infoagepub.com

kick-in-the-ass advice and direction I needed to become serious about doing research. Actually, John used to wake me from my hung-over stupor on Saturday mornings when I would be sleeping on three chairs in my office and get me going on research (preparing materials, running subjects). Sure, I also sought the advice, both solicited and unsolicited, of Kulhavy and Stock, who always directed me appropriately. But it was John who served as my mentor and savior while I was at ASU. To this day, we remain good friends.

Over the next year I would spend most of my time working on research projects with Kulhavy's team and other faculty as well. I worked with Helmstadter on a project that was eventually published in the *School Library Media Quarterly* (my first publication!). The atmosphere on the third floor of Payne Hall was great. Several grad students were always around, including Jim Webb (formerly at Kent State), Sean Mulvenon (UNLV), and Joanne Curran (retired from SUNY Oneonta). Looking back, I regret that I didn't take more advantage of the opportunities for mentoring that were available at ASU. Gene Glass would often chat with me informally when I had an office in the Farmer Building. I had no idea who this goofy professor was who said he grew up in Lincoln, Nebraska. Gene would often buy a few pitchers of beer for our group of grad students when he would find us hanging out at the Warehouse, a local bar. If I would have only had the sense to take a course or two from Gene and learn from him!

Dave Berliner was another person whom I had an opportunity to work with. I met with him one day to discuss research interests. I was stupid in thinking that I already had a full plate working with Kulhavy and Stock so I passed on working with Berliner. So, my memories of ASU with regards to mentoring are mixed. Sure, I got valuable knowledge from Kulhavy, Stock, and Behrens, but I also missed golden opportunities to work with other established scholars.

In Spring 1990, Bill Stock asked me if I wanted to go to AERA in Boston. I said yes but told him that I didn't have the money (just like the year before when Kulhavy had asked me to go to San Francisco). He said that he didn't ask me if I had enough money, just did I want to go. I said yes and Stock added me as a presenter in a symposium he had organized. The paper I would present wasn't even mine. Another grad student, Sue Faykus, was supposed to present it but couldn't attend AERA. The paper was on boxplot displays—something I knew nothing about. Nevertheless, thanks to Bill Stock, I was going to Boston. Back then, ASU did pretty well in terms of supporting grad student travel. I got $400 from the Graduate School, $300 from the dean's office and $150 from the department. Can you imagine, $850 for a grad student to present a paper that wasn't even mine? When I worked at the University of South Dakota in 1997–98, the annual travel budget for a faculty member in the Department of Educational Psychology was $300.

Kulhavy heard I was going to AERA and asked where I planned to stay. I told him that I was planning to stay at a cheaper outside hotel and take a taxi to the conference hotels each day, since it was too late to get a room at the conference hotels. Then Kulhavy did something quite generous. He told me that I could stay in a suite at one of the conference hotels with a bunch of other faculty and grad students. I would get a chance to meet some of the big names in learning and cognition and save money. I gladly accepted. Helping poor grad students is a great thing.

CHAPTER 7

HOW TO SAVE MONEY
ON LODGING

Conference hotels in large cities typically charge $200–$300 per evening. Add to this all the taxes and a four-night stay at AERA will likely run well over $1,000. How can a grad student or faculty member at a smaller university afford this? I have some suggestions.

First, don't be afraid to look at hotel options other than those listed on the AERA program site. When I attended AERA in Denver years back, I noticed that there was a Hilton Garden Inn right across the street from the Convention Center that was not listed among the "AERA" hotels. I booked a room there for cheaper than most of the other hotels. Today, many folks look at Airbnb options. But try to sleep close to the major events (receptions, etc.). You don't want to be walking back to your room over long distances after a successful night at the receptions. Believe me.

Second, go cheap. When I attended my first AERA meeting in Boston in 1990, my lodging costs were $40 per night. How did I do this? Well, I stayed at the NCIC suite. What is NCIC and why does Dan use annoying acronyms? Sorry. NCIC is the National Consortium for Instruction and Cognition. It was started back in 1970 by four of Dick Anderson's grad students at the University of Illinois. They simply wanted to do what I have said is the main purpose of attending AERA: to network and meet the top people in your field. To do so, they pooled their very limited funds and rented a suite rather than a room. There, they hosted after-reception parties—usually after 9 P.M. when the other receptions ended. Smart move—lots of people would like the fun to continue after 9 P.M. They offered top-shelf hooch and a place for seasoned and newer researchers to meet, drink, and converse. It was a brilliant idea, and the group is still going today. I make it a point to stop by "the suite" each year just to pay my respects to the spirit of this group.

Back at the AERA conference in Boston in 1990 (my first), I stayed at the suite. Now, it was not five-star accommodations, although it was in a five-star hotel. Those expecting otherwise will be disappointed. I did not have a room nor a bed. In fact, a few mornings I awoke to find women arriving to attend some of the morning research sessions that NCIC also held in the suite. I scrambled to grab my clothes and tried to get an available shower. All the towels were used by that time so I did what any industrious grad student would do—I took down some of the terry cloth curtains and used those. I can still hear Kulhavy when he walked in one morning to see our state of squalor. "Boys, this is good living."

It was simply a great experience. I stayed up late each evening and met the people whose research I had been reading in grad school. John Guthrie, Dick Anderson, Bob Gagne, Dave Berliner, and so forth. They were rock stars to me. In return for the reduced lodging rate, I had to, along with other grad students, sneak in alcohol each day in suitcases for that evening's gathering. No sweat. I had been doing that for years when I lived in the dorms. Well-practiced. So, my early grad student lodging experiences were great. Cheap lodging and great networking.

For those of you who do not embrace such a Kerouac lifestyle and want a guaranteed mattress each night, I suggest rooming with 3–5 other grad students. You can fit four people in two beds. You can also squeeze in a roll-away bed or bring an air mattress or two. This can greatly reduce the expenses. Then, when you get your first job out of grad school and are making a salary, you will appreciate sleeping in a room with fewer people. But be sure to pay it forward. Invite your grad students to stay in your room for free. I have done so every place I have worked. Help them out. It's the thing to do. Besides, they may give you their drink tickets and guide you back to your room at the end of the evening.

CHAPTER 8

MY FIRST AERA— BOSTON, 1990

I was on the same four-hour flight from Phoenix to Boston as Kulhavy when we left on Easter Sunday, 1990. I remember talking with Kulhavy about staying at the suite as we waited to claim our luggage. Some friends who had moved to Boston from Iowa gave me a ride to the hotel and I phoned the room that was registered under the name of Mike Royer. No one was there so I left a message saying I was one of Kulhavy's students and I was going to be staying in the room. I would be waiting in the lobby. This was about 5:00 P.M. After about six hours and about four more attempted phone calls, I was getting quite discouraged that no one was at the room, and I had no place to sleep. The hotel management wasn't buying my story that I was supposed to be staying at the room. Fortunately, Gerald Helmstadter found me in my desperate state and offered to let me sleep on the floor in his room for the night. Helmstadter was a great person. The next day, I showed up at the suite only to learn that I was a running joke among some of the NCIC folks. It turned out that Mike Royer and the other people rooming at the suite had been attending the NCIC presession until late in the evening and weren't expecting anyone to be coming to the suite that evening. Mike got back to the room late and listened to all of my messages. You can imagine how I felt that next day when I was introduced to Mike, and he got a big smile on his face. The worst part of it was that I embarrassed Kulhavy by saying that I was one of his students.

Bloody Mary for the AERA Attendee's Soul, pp. 27–29
Copyright © 2022 by Information Age Publishing
www.infoagepub.com

After getting over the awkward introductions, I found the suite to be a very good place for a grad student. I got to meet and talk to the same people whose articles and books I had been reading for the past year. I was most excited to meet Dick Anderson. Dick's experiments in the late 70s were some of the cleverest I had seen. The opportunity to talk with him about those studies was the equivalent of a young baseball fan talking to Mickey Mantle.

The thing that impressed me most about Dick is that he never talked down to me like many other less famous people. When he asked how I was associated with NCIC, I told him that Kulhavy had invited me to stay at the suite. Dick immediately began introducing me to people as his "grandson," meaning that because Kulhavy was his student, and thinking that I was Kulhavy's student, there was a family tie between us. I've attended every AERA/NCIC conference since my first one in Boston in 1990 and every time I see Dick, he always spends some time talking to me and giving me valuable advice.

NCIC is an organization that is similar to the Royal Family. Members are proud of the fact that they are direct "descendents" of Dick Anderson. In fact, to be a member of NCIC, you have to be able to trace your "lineage" to Dick or be sponsored by someone who has that lineage. I discovered this requirement in 1991 when I was no longer a student at ASU. I had joined NCIC as a student affiliate in 1990 and was sending in my dues for the 1991 conference. Don Cunningham sent me an e-mail stating that I needed someone to sponsor me, or I couldn't keep my student member status. Fortunately, John Behrens was a member and he sponsored me. This process of finding a sponsor every year seemed a bit peculiar to me. I stayed at the suite, made beer runs, tended bar, slept on the floor, and paid my share of the room but I was still treated like an outsider. I guess this wouldn't have occurred if I had been Kulhavy's student. But I was never Kulhavy's student. He invited me to stay at the suite, but he never chaired my dissertation—a requirement for lineage to the Dick Anderson bloodline.

Kulhavy told me before we left for AERA that he would be leaving ASU in the fall and that I should transfer to another school. He also told me that I could apply to Florida State University (FSU) and follow him there. I contacted Marcy Driscoll and she said that I was welcome to apply for admission and an assistantship at FSU. But it was not certain that Kulhavy would be hired. I was not going to go to FSU with no assistantship and what if Kulhavy would not be there? It turned out that Kulhavy ended up staying at ASU. I probably should have just applied to FSU and gone there if accepted. It would have been great to work with Marcy and Bob Gagne. And two of my good friends, Bryan and Marlynn Griffin, were grad students at FSU at that time and I'm sure we would have had fun.

When I was in Boston, I shopped for grad schools to pursue my doctoral degree. I attended a University of Michigan reception, and someone offered to fly me to Ann Arbor to interview for the educational psychology program. What an idiot I was to never pursue that! I was likely too drunk to remember the person's name and too embarrassed the next day to track him down (I think it was the late Paul Pintrich). I spoke with Tom Andre about attending Iowa State. Tom was interested and told me to apply. I also found Ken Kiewra at a session and was surprised that he remembered me so well. I asked him if he had any assistantships available. Ken offered me an assistantship on the spot. Since Tom couldn't do that and I wanted to decide where I was going, I accepted the offer from Nebraska and left ASU with a master's degree in May 1990. Again, I wonder what it would have been like to work with Tom and Gary Phye had I gone to Iowa State University.

I dated an ASU undergrad, Sheri Adolph, during the last two weeks I was in Arizona. Sheri then visited me in Iowa twice that summer and we agreed that we wanted to be together. She should transfer from ASU to Nebraska. A year later we were married, and Sheri completed her special education degree at University of Nebraska. I am very fortunate to have married a woman who is able to give me honest and critical feedback and keep me grounded. If I had my way, we would have worked on many projects together, but we also felt that we should separate ourselves to avoid leaving the impression that one of us is the brains behind it all (which would certainly be Sheri!).

CHAPTER 9

HOW TO SAVE MONEY ON TRAVEL

As mentioned previously, the AERA conference can easily cost over $2,000 to attend. I've already given you tips on saving money on food, drinks, and lodging. Travel is another major expense. Back in 1995 when AERA was held in New Orleans and I worked at Mississippi State University—only 300 miles away, I decided I would save big bucks on flights and drive to the conference instead. When Sheri and I got to our hotel on Canal Street, I needed to park for the five-day stay. Well, parking was over $50 per day so they gouged me pretty good. So much for driving unless you can find a cheap remote place to park.

Now, I'm no travel agent, but I can tell you a thing or two about booking flights. When AERA opens up registration for the conference, the website usually mentions that attendees can get up to 5–10% off airfares if they book through United or Delta. Don't do it. You can always find cheaper flights using a site like Travelocity or Priceline. Or check Southwest or JetBlue. If the cheapest flight is on one of the AERA-approved airlines, go directly to their website and book it. What if your university requires you to go with their approved travel agent? No problem. Just find your preferred cheap flight before and tell the agent what you want. And be sure to book early. If the conference is in April and you wait until spring break, you won't find many cheap options.

Once you arrive at the airport, the absolute most expensive way to get to your hotel is by taxi. The only times I use taxis these days is if I am in a real hurry and someone else is picking up the tab. Otherwise, a rideshare like Uber and Lyft is cheaper, but still much more expensive than using public transportation. The hotel shuttles are the worst traveling experience because although they are a bit cheaper than taxi or rideshare, you stop at many hotels along the way and ride in a cramped van for a long time. Much better to opt for light rail if available. When I go to Chicago and need to be frugal, I hop on the L. You can get within a few blocks of any hotel for about $5 total. The same is true in Atlanta and New York City.

If you are afraid of trains and simply want the comfort of a rideshare, then at least share the ride with someone who is going to the same hotel or within a block or two of your hotel. This cuts the cost dramatically. If you aren't traveling with such a person, look for people on the plane who are reading the AERA program on their mobile device. (AERA stopped mailing the printed program to attendees a few years ago. I guess they couldn't afford the $5 postal fee, although they continue to increase the already overpriced dues and registration costs yearly.) Then sidle up next to them at baggage claim and suggest sharing a ride. This may be a good networking opportunity or even a way to meet your future life partner.

When AERA was held in San Antonio in 2017, I had no travel money whatsoever. Fortunately, I lived only 100 miles away, so I drove to the conference. But what about parking? I parked at a friend's house in the suburbs, and he drove me downtown and also picked me up the last day. That's a huge solid. What about lodging? I simply emailed my buddies and asked if I could crash in their room for free. I offered to bring an air mattress so they wouldn't have to get a bigger room or pay for a rollaway. A few of them allowed me to stay for free on different nights. What about conference registration—which is ridiculously high? (Have I already mentioned that? I can't mention it enough.) Well, I simply borrowed my friends' badge when they were not using it to attend sessions, receptions, and so forth. Food and drink? Well, you've already read my strategies. Suffice it to say that I successfully attended AERA in 2017 and my wife was impressed with my frugality. Perhaps impressed is a strong word. Is shaking her head the same as impressed?

CHAPTER 10

NEBRASKA ACT II

The three years I spent at Nebraska as a grad student from 1990 to 1993 were very productive in terms of conducting research. I got to work with Ken Kiewra, Roger Bruning, and the late Gregg Schraw—a brand-new Assistant Professor hired in 1990. Those three people made up one of the best learning/cognition programs in the country. And I am proud that I took the initiative to be mentored by all three instead of making the earlier mistake at ASU. The work I did at Nebraska was very different than what I had done at ASU. I worked independently for the most part and ran numerous studies. I read research articles until 3:00 in the morning. I found that by going through the major journals (*Journal of Educational Psychology*, *Contemporary Educational Psychology*, etc.) over the past 10 or so years, I got a sense of what topics I was interested in that also matched where the field was going. I also immersed myself in cognitive psychology journals and books. The coursework I took was ok, but for the most part I learned my field by reading independently. I still believe that grad students should take this approach. Never believe that coursework is sufficient. Always read heavily outside of the classroom.

In 2000 at AERA, I spoke with some of the current grad students at Nebraska and they told me that I enjoyed a notorious reputation. It seems that the students thought that I never studied as a grad student and wrote my dissertation in only three months. They were right on both accounts. I didn't spend much time studying for exams and I proposed my dissertation in January and finished it in April of 1993. But I wasn't sacrificing course-

Bloody Mary for the AERA Attendee's Soul, pp. 33–35
Copyright © 2022 by Information Age Publishing
www.infoagepub.com
33

work to enjoy leisurely pursuits. Instead, I was running subjects in the computer lab or in the library reading books or journals. Just ask Sheri— she lived with me during those three years at Nebraska and can attest to my insane behavior of reading so much.

In 1993, I graduated with my PhD. When I began applying for assistant professor positions, I had a measly three publications—none of which were first author publications, and a handful of presentations. My only strength was probably teaching experience as I had taught about 20 undergrad classes. Like an idiot, I applied for every advertised position that I felt I was remotely qualified for. In all, I think I applied to 56 openings. The rejection letters poured in before anyone offered to interview me. I first received a call from William Patterson College in New Jersey. I learned that they would reimburse me for my travel expenses only if I accepted the job if they offered. No thanks. They were out. Next, I was invited to interview at the College of Saint Rose, a very small school that had a master's program in educational psychology. To date, this was the worst interview I have ever experienced. I am now certain that they must have already decided on a candidate when I arrived. A faculty member picked me up at the airport and dumped me off at my hotel on a Saturday evening. No dinner, nothing. The next day, I had to spend the entire Sunday trapped in my hotel until someone picked me up for dinner. There was two feet of snow on the ground, and I had to walk several blocks to find a place for lunch. At my interview talk, the dean read a newspaper and there were only two other faculty present! To top things off, someone took me to the airport two hours before my flight, which was delayed several hours. Yes, in 1993, it was unheard of to arrive at the airport that early.

I was very discouraged when I got home but my hopes brightened when SUNY Oneonta and Ball State University (BSU) called. I did both interviews as part of the same trip and the schools split my airfare. Oneonta had a four-course teaching load. Nelson Dubois and Dick Staley were good friends of mine and I know I could have been successful there. The problem was that Sheri wanted to attend grad school in school psychology and there was no such program at Oneonta. BSU was an excellent interview, and their school psychology program was APA accredited. They even wanted me to go through John Glover's files to see what I could do with some data he had collected right before he died. I really liked BSU and it seemed as though my search was over. I flew to Mississippi State University (MSU) the next week thinking that there was no way in hell I would take the job. The interview went well and the Department Head, Bill Graves, practically offered me the job during the exit interview. I told him that I would need to talk things over when I got home.

Sheri was shocked when I told her I liked MSU. She was a bit angry because I'm sure she didn't want to go through any more decisions. In a few days, BSU called and made me an offer. I told them I was flattered but needed a few days to think it over. MSU called on the final day BSU needed a decision. It was a very difficult decision. MSU was offering $500 more in salary, but BSU had a better school psych program for Sheri. Yes, $500 does not seem like much today but back then, a $30,000 salary is a bit less than what we make today. BSU also committed to a three-year assistantship for Sheri. After thoroughly talking it over, I called Bill Graves to decline and then called the dean at BSU and told him I would accept. Minutes after I hung up the phone, Bill Graves called and told me they would give me a two-course teaching load for one-year, match the assistantship offer for Sheri, and give me another $1,000 in salary. Now we were having second thoughts! After a half hour of discussion, I decided to call the dean at BSU to ask for another day to decide. I told him what MSU had offered. Well, he got pretty angry with me. I believe he said that if salary was the only thing keeping me from coming to BSU, perhaps I didn't want to be there. I told him I agreed and thanked him. I called Bill Graves and accepted his offer. Did I treat BSU badly? Perhaps. But to this day, I have never regretted my decision.

CHAPTER 11

HOW TO SAVE MONEY
AT THE EXHIBITS

The AERA Exhibit Hall is a wonderful place to visit. It's like a shopping mall for nerdy academics. In fact, during the conference I usually spend some time there each day. It is a great place to run into people I want to see. Beyond that, most publishers are there and if you are shopping for books to use in your classes, you can browse at your leisure. If you have an idea for a book, schedule time with a publisher. Better yet, schedule lunch. It will be free.

Every year, I always have young faculty members or grad students come up to me during the conference and attempt to impress me with the great deal they got on a book they bought at the exhibits. They were able to purchase the normally priced $150 book for "only" $120 as they got a huge discount. Then, their face drops as I ask them why they simply did not request an examination or instructor copy. They reply that because this book does not really fit as a required book for the undergraduate course they teach, they did not feel right about requesting an instructor copy. I then tell them that any book fits. They just need to fill out the form and make up a title for the course and say there are at least 20 students who will enroll. NEVER spend your own money on books at the AERA conference. And be sure to pick up plenty of free crap at the publishers' booths. I used to allow my kids to choose a few items (pens, foam stress relievers, etc.) when I would return home as a peace offering for being gone a few days. But keep the foam pencils. They are useful as reception ice breakers.

Bloody Mary for the AERA Attendee's Soul, pp. 37–37
Copyright © 2022 by Information Age Publishing
www.infoagepub.com
37

CHAPTER 12

MISSISSIPPI STATE

In the summer of 1993, I sold my motorcycle and Monte Carlo and we packed up everything we owned into a small U-Haul and drove to Starkville, Mississippi. MSU has a great faculty housing system where new faculty can live close to campus for a very low cost. We rented a two-bedroom duplex for $280 a month. No trip to Mississippi was needed that summer to look for housing and we were able to get on our feet financially those first two years. At MSU I met two new professors in the school psychology program who were very much die-hard behaviorists. Their names? Skinner and Watson, of course. Chris Skinner and Steuart Watson were very influential in helping me to be successful as a researcher. They did this not by serving as mentors or collaborating with me but rather they modeled good researcher behavior. I remember going to the office on Saturday and Sunday mornings with Chris Skinner to work on papers. This was the only way to get ahead of the backlog of data I had been collecting since grad school. Once I had children, those days of weekend office visits were over!

Starkville did not have much in the way of cultural attractions or a reputation of being a great college town in 1993. It was very much a Bible-Belt town where most students go home on the weekends and Sunday mornings are spent in church, not nursing hangovers. We had great times in Starkville because we made friends with other faculty couples who felt as displaced as we were. Weekend evenings were spent drinking and arguing over the cognitive psychology-behaviorism debates. These were healthy discussions and over time we (the behaviorists and me) came to realize that

Bloody Mary for the AERA Attendee's Soul, pp. 39–40
Copyright © 2022 by Information Age Publishing
www.infoagepub.com

we had much more in common than different. For one thing, the theories used to explain behavior were not nearly as important as how convincing the evidence was. We also were interested in interventions that would change behavior with the ultimate goal being to help students learn more effectively. Skinner, Watson, and I remain good friends to this day because we all focus more on outcomes rather than theories.

I had the good fortune of meeting and working with other good people at MSU. Jim Weber was an associate dean of research and he helped me in so many areas by being an excellent mentor. Andy Katayama was my only true grad student. Andy is a tireless worker who collaborated with me on about seven projects during the three years he was at MSU. Andy influenced my life probably way more than I influenced him because he is such an outstanding person.

I also began to collaborate with researchers at other universities since there were not many educational psychology faculty at MSU who were interested in conducting research. Marlynn Griffin was one of those persons. I e-mailed Marlynn one day to register for NCIC and she offered to take care of my sponsorship problem. Marlynn was a full member and she sponsored me. We chatted over telephone and e-mail and decided to collaborate on some mutual interests. I have found Marlynn to be a very valuable research partner. Her writing skills far surpass mine and she is a very hard worker. And she was able to publish while managing a family and teaching a heavy course-load. Marlynn has certainly served as a mentor to me in terms of modeling excellent scholar and teacher behavior.

Joel Levin was another person I contacted while at MSU. Joel had served as editor of the *Journal of Educational Psychology* when I submitted my dissertation there. I came to know Joel quite well as I ended up revising my paper six times before it was accepted. When I asked Joel if he would be interested in co-authoring a paper with me, he surprised me by accepting. I truly believe that I have learned more from working with Joel Levin early in my career than I learned from my entire grad school experience.

CHAPTER 13

WORKING WITH GRAD STUDENTS

Let's shift to some unsolicited advice concerning working with grad students. If you work at a Research I university, then you, as a faculty member, are expected to engage graduate students in scholarly research pursuits that result in presentations at national research conferences, such as AERA, and publications in top refereed journals, such as the *Journal of Educational Psychology*. If you are a current graduate student, then faculty members should be working with you. In a nutshell, this is the most important activity at a Research I institution. This is crucial for students who wish to be considered for tenure track faculty positions at Research I institutions upon graduation. I have seen too many students who enter graduate school with great potential only to realize four to five years later that they spent their time pursuing and perfecting activities that are less important. These activities include, but are not limited to, coursework, employment, and endless hours of meetings. Each of these activities may be necessary to graduate but ultimately can be counterproductive if research productivity suffers. For this reason, I unapologetically push graduate students to spend more time being productive and to prioritize the many activities on the graduate student plate.

To be competitive for tenure track faculty positions at the top research universities, grad students should strive for at least three publications in nationally refereed journals in their field, perhaps serving as first author on at least one, and present at least 10 papers at national and regional

Bloody Mary for the AERA Attendee's Soul, pp. 41–43
Copyright © 2022 by Information Age Publishing
www.infoagepub.com
All rights of reproduction in any form reserved.

research conferences. This level of productivity does not happen overnight. In fact, it requires 4–5 years of work. This means that the brand-new grad student hits the ground running and does not waste a year or two "finding an area of research."

When I was at the University of Texas at Austin (UT-Austin), an undergraduate stopped by my office one day and told me he would be applying to our graduate program the following year. He also asked if he could be involved in some of my research projects while he was still an undergrad, so that he could hit the ground running. Such foresight is rare. That student, Michael Mayrath, went on to do a two-year post doc at Harvard after he received his PhD.

I believe it is best for new grad students to join research teams and serve as coauthors until they are prepared to lead a study. Sometimes first-year students lead studies, but this is rare. Michael Sweet, now at Northeastern University, comes to mind as an exception to this rule. He arrived at UT-Austin ready to conduct a series of studies on team-based learning. Students should not worry if they do not have a great idea; instead, they should realize that the best way for ideas to emerge is to begin collecting data and running studies. As part of the research process, students will also constantly devour research articles that appear in the top journals of their field. My wife likes to tell people how I was usually up until three in the morning reading research articles when I was in grad school.

Each fall semester it is my goal to have an open meeting (anyone is welcome to attend) where I lay out all the current research studies with which I am involved. Because grad students lead almost all of these studies, I ask them to give a status report and they may invite others to become part of the team. Sometimes studies are almost completed and there is really no room for another team member at that stage. Students are welcome to observe the process from that point on. Other studies are simply at the conception stage, and we discuss how many team members are still needed and what roles are needed. We always discuss, in the very first meeting of a particular research team, who is going to lead the study and serve as first author. We discuss other roles and authorship order. We discuss our goals for the project, such as an AERA presentation to be submitted the coming summer and finally a journal to which we hope to submit the completed study. I find that when these things are discussed early, rather than later, fewer problems result. Let me repeat that on almost all projects with which I am involved, grad students serve as first author, and I delegate myself to last author—if my contribution warrants authorship at all. There are some faculty members who rarely have students as first authors. I don't believe this is the best way to train and help students.

I'm not a big fan of engaging in research projects that require more than a year's worth of data collection. If we are conducting a program of research with multiple experiments, then perhaps two semesters and a summer will be required to collect all the data. But I tend to lose interest if studies drag on forever. I've heard horror stories of students who agree to work with a research team and five years later the study is still not completed. What is worse, the student has virtually nothing to show for the effort, except maybe a ninth authorship on a regional conference presentation. I strive to ensure that students who work with me will not have those experiences.

That said, there is no guarantee that manuscripts we submit for publication will be accepted. I've had numerous papers go through several rounds of revisions and journals to which we submit. The process can be frustrating. However, such is the nature of publishing in education. Ask any of the top-producing researchers and they will share the same stories. That is why it is best to have at least four research studies going at the same time. This increases your chances for a level of productivity that will get you the job and keep the job. Students should choose their projects and team members wisely. Grad school is not a good time to work with someone "just to be nice." Spending countless hours discussing research with others and never publishing is to be avoided.

For the most part, grad students who work with me have worked hard and impressed me with their abilities and work ethic. Occasionally, there will be one team member that is on everyone's complaint list. Such students usually drop the ball more than once and slow down the team. I have never kicked such students off of teams. However, once the project is complete, I simply don't invite the student to participate again. These students are not on my list when it comes to writing letters of recommendation.

Regardless of these precautions, it is still important to work with a variety of faculty and other grad students. Faculty members need something on which to base their letters of recommendation and fellow grad students can serve as a support network that can get one through the process. I encourage students to learn about other faculty members' current projects and to work with as many as possible. But again, I caution that students should not spend too much of their time chasing research projects that have little chance of fruition. Avoid working with faculty who, rather than being good mentors, turn out to be dementors (Robinson, 2011). As Remus Lupin explained to Harry Potter:

> Dementors are among the foulest creatures that walk this earth. They infest the darkest, filthiest places, they glory in decay and despair, they drain peace, hope, and happiness out of the air around them.... Get too near a Dementor and every good feeling, every happy memory will be sucked out of you. If it can, the Dementor will feed on you long enough to reduce you to something like itself ... soulless and evil. You will be left with nothing but the worst experiences of your life. (Rowling, 1999)

CHAPTER 14

SOUTH DAKOTA

In the fall of 1996, my daughter, Kylie, was born in Mississippi and I saw my limited time for research become much more limited. No regrets here— Kylie's arrival had a sobering effect on me (literally) in terms of my lifestyle. I came to understand where my family and job are sequenced in the priorities of my life. I'll always strive to work hard in terms of teaching, research, and service. But the one job I remain most focused on today is being a husband and father.

About this time, Sheri began applying for internships and I began looking for teaching positions near the internship sites. If you get a PhD in school psychology, you hope to do your internship at an APA-accredited site. There were no accredited sites within 100 miles of Starkville, Mississippi. So, we knew that we would eventually have to leave MSU. To be honest, we would never have sent our children to school in Mississippi. We love our children too much to subject them to that kind of environment. Sheri ended up getting an internship at Boys Town near Omaha, Nebraska. I applied for a one-year leave of absence from MSU and looked for work near Omaha. There were a few teaching positions in education and psychology at small colleges near and around Omaha, but I never got even a nibble. I applied to teach public school as I had received a Nebraska teaching certificate. It turns out that I was not eligible to teach because I had not kept up with my professional development requirements. I had taught courses that qualified as professional development credits when I was at MSU but since I had not taken the courses, they would not count.

Bloody Mary for the AERA Attendee's Soul, pp. 45–47
Copyright © 2022 by Information Age Publishing
www.infoagepub.com

I finally decided to look for construction jobs as I would have to feed my family. I never considered staying in Mississippi and driving 900 miles to see my wife and baby once a month. I would have never made it through the misery of missing the two people I loved the most.

Andy Katayama had been applying for jobs that spring of 1997 and had interviewed at the University of South Dakota (USD). Andy wasn't too excited about working at USD and, becoming desperate, I knew that Vermillion, South Dakota was only 140 miles from Omaha. I asked Andy if he would mind if I inquired about the job and he said no. When I called Frank Main, the department chair, he said that they had already hired someone. I told Frank my situation and that I could teach statistics. He said that earlier that day one of the statistics professors submitted his resignation and they needed someone for that coming academic year. I sent Frank my vita and in two weeks, I met with him and the dean for an informal interview. I was hired as a temporary professor at $8,000 less than what I was making at MSU.

The year I spent at USD was good for me professionally but difficult for me personally. I would leave Omaha at 8:00 A.M. on Monday mornings and drive two hours to Vermillion. I slept in a dorm Monday, Tuesday and Wednesday evenings and left USD at noon on Thursdays to go back to Omaha. Fridays were my day to spend with my baby girl and the weekends were family time. Although my heart ached during the week, the weekends were great. Frank Main was very kind to allow me to spend only three and a half days a week at my job. It's funny writing this over 20 years later. If most of our faculty came to work 3.5 days a week, it would be much more than they do now. While I was at USD, I worked over 12 hours a day. There was nothing else for me to do there. I had data from several studies that had not been written up when I was at MSU. At USD, I had nothing but time and managed to send off about six papers for publication. In a sense, USD was like a sabbatical for me in that I collected very little data but wrote up everything I had lying around.

Frank Main proved to be a valuable mentor for me. He helped me obtain a site license for SPSS the first month I was there. USD had two graduate stats courses but no statistical software. We managed to get money from the vice president for research, and the deans of education and arts and sciences. I don't know how I would have taught advanced statistics had we not obtained SPSS. Frank also helped me get a $500 research travel grant to go to AERA in San Diego in 1998. As I mentioned earlier, each faculty member had $300 in travel money for the year, so getting the $500 extra made San Diego almost affordable. Frank was able to work wonders. He taught me how to find money.

While at USD, I applied for several jobs where there might be a possibility of two openings in school psych and ed psych. I was invited to seven interviews that year: Illinois State, Georgia Southern, University of Missouri-Kansas City, University of Nebraska-Omaha, University of South Dakota, University of Louisville, and Penn State. I never received an offer at the first five interviews. Bryan Griffin fought valiantly for me at Georgia Southern University but the faculty selected an internal candidate. Funny how things work out, but that same person who took my job at Georgia Southern ended up taking my old job at Louisville two years later! With all the failed attempts, suffice it to say that the spring of 1998 was about the worst I have ever felt about my qualifications as a professor. I thought no one wanted me.

What I learned from my interview experience over those three years is that you should take care to interview only at universities where you are a good fit. I had always thought that a tier two, three, or four school would consider themselves fortunate to land a person who was able to publish in the top journals. Not so. At those universities most people do not place great emphasis on research and publishing. I was viewed as being threatening by many faculty according to persons at those schools I spoke with after my interviews.

CHAPTER 15

WHERE TO PUBLISH?

I used to teach a doctoral-level research design course when I was at Colorado State University. As part of the course requirements, I had students meet with their advisor and come up with a list of the top 5–10 journals in their field. Then I had the students complete a brief report about each journal including the *Web of Science* impact factor, whether it was open-access only, whether there was a fee to publish, and so forth. My department chair contacted me a few weeks into the semester and said that a few faculty members had complained about my assignment. They were either struggling to come up with the list of journals or were upset about the information I was requesting about each journal. It turns out that these faculty had given the students journal lists that contained quite a few journals that either registered no impact factor or were considered open access.

Quantity is certainly important when it comes to research. Not many Research I universities will award you tenure with under 10 journal articles. At the same time, quality must also be considered. Years ago, when I was new to the field, we didn't have what are now called open access journals. Instead, we called journals that charged publishing fees "vanity press" journals. Publishing in such journals didn't count for much. I confess that I was introduced to this concept by submitting something once to a reading journal—maybe it was *Reading Horizons*. I thought I had done my due diligence and researched the journal. It appeared legitimate and it was included among the periodicals in the Mississippi State University library. I was somewhat surprised when I received a favorable decision letter about

Bloody Mary for the AERA Attendee's Soul, pp. 49–51
Copyright © 2022 by Information Age Publishing
www.infoagepub.com

a week after submission. I thought to myself, "wow, I must be getting really good at this whole publishing thing!" Much to my dismay, as I read more of the acceptance letter, I found a part where it mentioned that I would be required to pay a "page fee." It turned out that I was going to have to dish out a few thousand dollars! I asked a few colleagues about this, and they smiled and said this was a vanity press journal. Such journals are notorious for accepting almost everything. More importantly, they count for nothing.

Nowadays, we call these vanity-press journals "open-access" journals. This sounds much better than the vanity label. Proponents claim that these journals are consistent with the idea that research should be "open," and everyone should be able to access it. In this way, more of our valuable research ideas get out there to be used by practitioners. Who would be against such a humanitarian effort?

The problem is that the low-quality issue remains. Some of these journals will send you an acceptance e-mail within milliseconds of receiving your submission. Others are worse and are called "predatory" open-access journals. These journals might be published in some 18-year-old guy's basement. And yes, this is a true example. I've had faculty who have had something accepted in one of these journals and actually come to me as their chair and request the publishing fees. Such faculty are certainly unique. It's similar to people who run into you with their car and ask you to pay for the damage to their car.

Contributing to this problem is the fact that at many universities the library will set aside funds to pay for publishing fees for faculty if they get something accepted in an open-access journal. Seems that most libraries are very driven by the idea of open-resources and think that publishing in open-access journals is consistent with this mission. It's not. Paying for the publishing fees is like buying a case of whiskey for an alcoholic.

Always strive to publish your work in the journals with the best reputation. These journals almost always register an impact factor which shows that their articles are being cited by other journals. I always get faculty members who argue that this particular steaming pile of $#@% journal is very well respected in the field even though it has no impact factor. I then ask them to prove it. Let me ask a few people in their field at top universities if it would make their top 10 list. I have yet to have anyone agree to gather this evidence.

It's similar to a young man telling you about his new girlfriend who he just met a few weeks ago. He is convinced that she is the one. The only thing bothering him is that whenever they spend time together, she charges him money. But she seems really nice though.

For those of you who wish to make your work more widely available to people outside of academia, you can still pay to publish and keep high standards. Almost all high-quality journals offer the opportunity to make your article "open-access" for a fee. It then becomes available to anyone. So, if you have the money, consider this option. I have done so a few times and found that it increases the numbers of consulting opportunities I get.

CHAPTER 16

LOUISVILLE AND TEXAS

In the spring of 1998, the University of Louisville (UofL) surprised me when they offered me a job. Granted, they were not a major research university. But their educational foundations department was in dire need of someone who could chair dissertations and because the department was dominated by older faculty who were quickly approaching retirement, I guess I was viewed as being minimally threatening. Ray Nystrand, the dean, even made a phone call and got Sheri an interview for a post doc in pediatric psychology. Sheri got the job. A tenure-track position for me and a post doc for Sheri in the same city. Not bad for two people looking for two jobs. Of course, Penn State called right before I accepted the job at UofL but there was not enough time to interview. Besides, they didn't have a spousal hire policy so there would be nothing for Sheri. One of my fellow grad students at Nebraska, Rayne Sperling, was eventually hired at Penn State and today is an associate dean.

The year we spent at UofL was mixed in terms of our happiness. It was difficult for our family because Sheri's post doc kept her quite busy with long hours. To top it off, she completed and defended her dissertation during that year. My advice to everyone: Never attempt to complete a dissertation while working over 50 hours per week with a toddler. I was able to be productive in my writing, but the downside was that there were few students or colleagues with whom I could collaborate, like most non-Research I schools. UofL is a commuter campus, but I did not expect the faculty to also be commuters. Each day I was at work, it was like a ghost

Bloody Mary for the AERA Attendee's Soul, pp. 53–55
Copyright © 2022 by Information Age Publishing
www.infoagepub.com

town on my floor of the education building. Faculty would come in to teach courses in the evenings and only visited their offices to get their things. Their offices were more like lockers. So, it was quiet, and I was able to do some writing, but the collegiality was missing, and I don't think I could have been happy at UofL.

We inquired about future employment possibilities for Sheri while we were in Louisville. We knew that her post doc would only last one year and she would have to find something by August of 1999. The College of Education was opening up a new early childhood research center and it was supposed to be interdisciplinary. Sheri applied for one of the two new faculty lines, but like most schools, UofL procrastinated on their search for a director and by the time they hired one, it was too late to interview for the faculty positions. I pestered Ray Nystrand about the openings repeatedly, but he did not want to act independently and hire Sheri. It was his last year as dean after 20 years and he did not want to make any midnight appointments. We sent out a few applications looking for two faculty positions again but weren't very confident that we would be successful.

I was invited to interview at the University of Nevada–Las Vegas (UNLV) in the spring of 1999. They also had a position opening in school psych and when we inquired, Sheri had made the short list. Encouraged, I flew to Vegas and met with Alice Corkill and Frank Dempster, two excellent faculty in the department. I thought the interview went very well and was shocked to learn that they were going to offer the job to someone else. I later learned that some of the faculty were threatened by me. The department chair told me that if it were up to her, she would hire me and the dean would have created a school psych position for Sheri. UNLV would have been a great place to work, and it makes me even more disappointed when I learned one year later that the department hired Ralph Reynolds, Gale Sinatra, and Gregg Schraw to give UNLV one of the nation's strongest learning programs.

I was also invited to interview at the University of Missouri–Columbia. Sheri was angry with me for accepting the interview because there was no advertised school psych opening. I argued that we had to take our chances that the dean would create a school psych position. Many universities now have spousal hire policies where they promise to create a position for a spouse if funding permits. I spoke with CarolAnne Kardash on the phone, and she encouraged me to interview, knowing that I would be asking for two positions. CarolAnne fought hard for me, and I was offered the job. Unfortunately, there would be no school psych position for Sheri, and I had to decline.

About a week later, Ed Emmer, the department chair at the University of Texas called me. They had already interviewed three people for a cognition/learning position, and I was next on their list. I told Ed up front that we were looking for two positions. He asked what area Sheri was in and when I told him, he said they happened to have an opening in school psychology. I faxed Sheri's vita and the next day Emmer invited us both to interview.

Texas had a notorious reputation in 1999 for not promoting its assistant professors. In fact, the past seven people who had gone up for tenure were denied. Moreover, several others left before ever going up for tenure. That made the positions we were interviewing for a bit scary. But two positions at Texas that may last only five years were better than only one position elsewhere. We also had interviews scheduled for two positions at Eastern Washington University but cancelled them when Texas offered us two jobs. Eastern Washington had two great people, Ron and Nancy Martella, and we hated to tell them that we were backing out. But they also had a 12-hour teaching load that is twice the load at Texas. Both are now at Purdue and Nancy is the dean.

I wrote most of my academic journey in 2000 after I had completed my first year at the University of Texas. At that time, we were very pleased with our decision. Our son, Austin Jacques was born in May 2000, and we had the daunting challenge of trying to raise two children and secure tenure. Well, 21 years have passed since then and I have more to tell. But that is another story and volume.

CHAPTER 17

RECRUITING GRAD STUDENTS

In 2007, I was making preparations to attend AERA in Chicago. I was, as usual, going to room with Andy Katayama. Andy told me that he was bringing a guy who would also room with us. His name was Camilo Guerrero, and he was an Air Force major who worked with him at the Academy in Colorado Springs. He said that Camilo was planning to attend graduate school that fall and had narrowed his choices to the Universities of Wisconsin and Texas.

I first met Camilo in person when they showed up at the hotel room the first day of the conference. Camilo was a high-energy, gung-ho, true-blue (Air Force term) kind of guy. He explained that he had received his masters from the University of Arizona and had taken classes from Joel Levin—my good friend and mentor. Now, here's the part where I become evil.

Camilo said he had discussed his options with Joel and that Joel was strongly encouraging him to go to Wisconsin, a place where Joel had spent 30 years as a faculty member. Well, I guess that stuck in my craw a bit. Sure, I realized that Wisconsin was a top educational psychology program, and it would be a fantastic place for Camilo to study. But I also thought we at the University of Texas weren't too bad ourselves. So, I decided then and there that I had a few days to close the sale and get Camilo to flip to Texas.

I had a few things working in my favor. Camilo was staying in my hotel room, so we had hours to talk. He was also accompanying Andy and me on our reception-hopping escapades. Honestly, I did not behave like the consummate professional that week. Instead, we laughed a lot like teenagers.

We also had a lot of Texas grad students attending AERA that year. Camilo was meeting and spending time with our outstanding current students. Although we couldn't convince Camilo that the faculty or reputation of Texas was better than Wisconsin, we did convince him that if he decided to join us, he would have a great time and be part of a culture where everyone valued research and inquiry. Wisconsin didn't stand a chance. This was like an illegal recruiting visit for college football. I was Barry Switzer.

Camilo enrolled at the University of Texas and graduated three years later. Like many of the students who worked with me, Camilo not only was part of my research team, but he also became my bike riding, tennis playing, wings eating companion on the weekends. I am confident he had a great experience. In the acknowledgments section of his dissertation, he wrote:

> I give special thanks to my advisor, Dr. Dan Robinson, who is the reason
> why I came to Texas in the first place! From our first meeting in Chicago,
> I knew that two good ol' Iowa boys could work together and still have fun
> throughout one's daunting journey of obtaining a dissertation.

I wish this story had a happy ending. Camilo went back to the Air Force Academy after receiving his PhD and was promoted to Lieutenant Colonel. He continued to teach. In 2016, he was diagnosed with stage four cancer. He fought a great battle and lasted just over two years. He left behind a wife and three young sons. I miss him dearly and will always remember with a smile his recruiting trip back in 2007. The lesson here is that working with grad students isn't simply about mentoring them academically. Invite them into your life. Make them a part of your academic family. Show them that an academic life can include many activities outside of the university. Make it fun.

CHAPTER 18

THE FIVE-TOOL FACULTY MEMBER

This book, if you didn't grasp it by now, is intended for grad students and those new or newer faculty who are interested in how to be successful, obtain tenure, and so forth. Such advice is bound to be idiosyncratic. But, if my own daughter or son were going into educational academia, this is the advice I would offer them.

In baseball, there is a term called the five-tool player. You can break this down into the five individual tools needed for baseball. In short, the five tools are: run, catch, throw, hit for average, hit for power. Ask older baseball fans for players who had all five tools and they will mention Willie Mays and Mickey Mantle. Some of the more recent players might include Ken Griffey Jr. and pre-steroids era Barry Bonds and Alex Rodriguez. Today's players might include Mike Trout and Bryce Harper.

It is important to note that most baseball players do not possess exceptional skills for all five tools. In fact, some do very well with four tools or less. For example, Babe Ruth in his latter playing days did not run as well as he did when he was younger (none of us do) but he was still productive to the team.

For those of you who are not baseball fans, forgive me for using baseball as an analogy, but I thought it might serve as a working model. A few years back, I attempted to draw an analogy between the five-tool baseball player and the five-tool faculty member. I restricted my definition of faculty

Bloody Mary for the AERA Attendee's Soul, pp. 59–61
Copyright © 2022 by Information Age Publishing
www.infoagepub.com

member to a tenure-line person at a Research I institution. Here are the five tools I selected:

Teaching. It is difficult to measure excellence in teaching. We are often left with solely using course instructor surveys (CIS). But we all know that just because you average a 4.9 out of 5 for "instructor effectiveness," this does not necessarily mean you were great. It might simply mean the students liked you and the grade they received. For such CIS data, as an administrator, I typically used them to raise red flags if there is trouble (e.g., unusually low ratings). I think such data is most useful if distributions of grades are also examined to show that the instructor is not giving out A's like candy. Perhaps the most useful bit of information for me is word of mouth. If students tell me how much they learned in a particular instructor's course, I feel good about that person's teaching. If that student is well-prepared to enter the next more difficult course, I am also impressed.

Advising/Mentoring. At a Research I institution, the main "work" for a faculty member is producing PhDs. These graduate students need to be well-prepared so that they can be successful at obtaining jobs and succeeding. The bulk of this training involves learning the ins and outs of research. Excellent advising involves preparing graduates that successfully compete for the top jobs. Their vitas are the best. They interview well. In short, they are ready for independent research with no safety net. How is this success measured? Successful advisors can point to the publication records of their advisees. They can point to successful grants their advisees have had funded (this is rare). Coauthoring journal publications with grad students is essential. Grad students should also present research at major conferences in their field. Finally, dissertations chaired by excellent advisors are quickly converted to manuscripts that are eventually published in top journals.

Grants/External Funding. Research I institutions thrive and survive on externally funded research. Indirect costs fund travel for faculty who are unsuccessful in getting grants and also small grant programs to assist beginning faculty. In this day and age, perhaps nothing is more important for universities than grant funding. That said, grants are difficult to obtain and rarely do a majority of department faculty receive funding. How then, does faculty earn their keep? Another way to bring in outside funds is to serve as evaluators or consultants on projects. If this is done without university affiliation, then no money comes into the university. However, if a faculty member creates a center where such work can be done, then money can come into the university to help fund graduate students. I should mention that the major purpose of external funding is to fund graduate students. Anything above and beyond that is gravy. If you want to work with grad students, the onus is on you to find ways to support them. If you are successful, you may be able to have your own lab with space for 5–10 grad students, post docs, and so forth.

Service. At first glance you may think I will refer to university and department committees here. No. I think such "in-house" service is necessary and we need to all chip in. But I am referring to external service here. By this I mean service to the field. Serving on editorial boards, serving as journal editor, and so forth. Perhaps leading a national research organization. Attending meetings and being visible. Much of this service is pro bono. But it is essential. When an editor sends you a paper to review as an ad hoc reviewer, there is no monetary reward. But you agree and do a good job. This type of service allows a field to survive. Anyone can serve on an "in-house" committee. But it reflects increasing stature and expertise to be invited to review, serve on boards, and serve as an editor.

Research. The measurable products of our labor are reflected in the scholarship we produce. There are several different levels of scholarship. Technical reports, encyclopedia entries, and so forth, represent the lower levels. Nonempirical presentations at state or regional conferences are also low level. Book chapters are usually by invitation and the review process is much less rigorous than for journals. A major book in one's area can be impressive. But then one must examine the publisher, the sales, etc. in determining quality. Perhaps the easiest indicator for scholarship is the journal article. Journals vary in quality. Some journals are open-access, web-based only and charge per page for publication. Such vanity press publications do not count for much. The top journals register what is known as impact factors. This means that articles in those journals are cited frequently in other respected journals. For one to possess the research tool, one has to consistently publish in top journals.

As a caveat, looking back at my 20+ years as a ball player, I mean faculty member, I'd say I came up short in the grants area. Sure, I had a couple, but that is similar to a pitcher in the National League accidently connecting for a few home runs when he occasionally bats. I continue to work on this deficit. But right now, I'm at best an overweight Babe Ruth. At worst, I'm John Kruk.

CHAPTER 19

RANTING ABOUT
THE FIELD OF EDUCATION

In the book *Fossil Men* (Pattison, 2021), paleoanthropologist Tim White rips his colleagues a new one at a conference. He says the field has gone to crap. Way too many poorly-trained PhDs are being flooded into the field each year who are ill-equipped to contribute. What's more, the majority don't want to go out and do fieldwork anymore. They simply want others to find and share their fossils so they can sit in their cozy laboratories and "analyze" the data.

This resonated with me. In my 28 years since obtaining my PhD, I see a similar trend in education. We produce way too many freshly-minted "scholars" who have few skills to contribute to the field. I understand the need to do qualitative research. But it seems that many are attracted to the methodology simply because they do not have the chops for statistics. As for writing ability, I sincerely miss my days at the University of Texas. I had doctoral students who were better writers than me. Editing their work was not a chore. Instead, it was an exercise in making me a better writer.

Beginning with my time at Colorado State, I have seen a real decline in writing ability in doctoral students. Going further back to my time at Mississippi State in the mid-90s, I witnessed K–12 principals and superintendents who could not write a complete sentence. In fact, in an educational leadership course syllabus was a topic: the comma. I'm not kidding. The

Bloody Mary for the AERA Attendee's Soul, pp. 63–64

PhD in education is now easier to obtain than a bachelor's in engineering, business, and so forth.

When I first read White's comments about armchair researchers who never go out and collect data, I thought of the push for effect size reporting that began over 20 years ago. The folks who called themselves meta-analysts wanted empirical researchers to make it easier for them to do their armchair "research." Don't get me wrong. Gene Glass is one of my good friends and a great mentor. I also greatly respect Larry Hedges, Harris Cooper, and so forth. But, like many pursuits, meta-analysis has been plagued by the laziness of several who abuse it. Rather than sit back and draw inappropriate generalizations about a field of study that you have never set foot in, get your ass out and collect some empirical data!

The same goes for the correlation/observational researchers out there. Most simply want to create the latest "instrument" that assesses a new self-_____ construct. Then they email the instrument to several students and run fancy statistical causal modeling analyses—even though there is absolutely no causality to be found whatsoever. This is classic armchair research. Shockingly, they find that their new construct correlates highly with other BS self-_____ constructs. And they all correlate with student achievement. Then they conclude that if teachers would only increase self-_____ in their students, achievement would increase. Of course, because they are correlated. Poppycock!

I have always prided myself on conducing intervention research—mainly experimental—where I randomly assign students to conditions. This allows me to pursue causal questions. I had long thought that I was one of the "good guys" who got my hands dirty in the "lab" of running experiments with college students. Only later did I discover that some scholars could easily look down on me as I had looked down on the armchair scholars.

My good friend, Sharon Vaughn, who is a rock star at the University of Texas, averages over 10 empirical articles and about $20 million in grant funding annually. She obtains money so that she can conduct experimental research in K–12 classrooms that really matters. I wonder how she would regard my usual day spent walking down the hallway from my office and collecting data in a computer lab using human fruit flies (subject pool students). There is armchair research, there is backyard research (mine), and there is boots-on-the-ground, front-line research by folks like Sharon.

So, the next time you feel like ranting, remember, there is always someone out there who is stronger, better-looking, works harder, and so forth. Just be happy you have a job.

CHAPTER 20

REVIEWING AND EDITING

As a beginning scholar, you may wonder how you will proceed through the ranks of being an ad hoc journal reviewer (which may get you an acknowledgement on a single page in the last issue of the journal in a given year) to being invited to serve on an editorial board (where you are listed on the masthead), to becoming an associate editor, and finally, serving as a journal editor. Well, it all begins with your introduction to the "field" when you become an author or coauthor on a journal publication.

Preceding your first experience as an author will be, hopefully, a ton of reading. My wife, Sheri, recalls during our first few years together when I was in grad school, I would stay up until 2 or 3 in the morning reading journal articles. Yes, I have now mentioned this three times in this book. It cannot be understated. Read! I wanted to get a feel for what is published and how it is published. I gained an understanding of the language and writing style. This led to pre-dissertation research that resulted in several conference presentations and a few journal publications. After I landed my first academic gig at Mississippi State, I e-mailed journal editors and volunteered to serve as an ad hoc reviewer, hoping that this would lead, someday, to receiving an invitation to serve on the board. I attached my vita and also described my areas of "expertise" in a few sentences. Eventually, a full 12 years after receiving my PhD, I was invited to serve as editor of *Educational Psychology Review* (EDPR). I served in that role for 10 years, and also as an associate editor for the *Journal of Educational Psychology* for seven years. As of summer, 2021, I am enjoying a break from 15 years straight of

Bloody Mary for the AERA Attendee's Soul, pp. 65–68
Copyright © 2022 by Information Age Publishing
www.infoagepub.com

handling manuscripts. It is also an appropriate time for me to reflect and offer some advice based on my experiences.

To explain my views and approach to being an editor, I will first describe a few personal experiences as an author very early in my career. My very first "first" author experience occurred in 1993 when I submitted a manuscript to *Contemporary Educational Psychology* (CEP). Ray Kulhavy was editor. Ray had taken over the journal in 1990 when it was almost "dead" in terms of submissions. To this day, I often point to this experience as being crucial in helping me become a productive researcher in terms of journal publications. Ray's initial decision letter to me was "major revisions, revise and resubmit." As a young author, when I first read these words, it was very discouraging, devastating, deflating, and so forth. But I eventually realized that the editor had, in fact, allowed me to slip my foot in the door, so to speak. I had been given a roadmap showing me how to get closer to an acceptance. The editor was essentially saying, if you do a good job revising the paper according to the reviewer concerns, I will consider this further. As an author, you simply cannot ask for more. Sure, there are the "accept as is," and "accept with minor revisions," but these initial decisions are rare. So, I tackled the revisions diligently, paying close attention to the reviewers' suggestions and making sure that I did not simply dismiss or pay lip service to the concerns. By doing so, my paper was strengthened and eventually accepted.

The "developmental" approach to editing espoused by Kulhavy is one that has stuck with me to this day as an editor. I try to imagine that the author is submitting to the journal for the very first time. I also imagine that the person is not filled with confidence about the chances of publication. A quick negative decision is affronting and may discourage them from submitting again. Likewise, if they have to wait a year to get a hurried, last-minute decision based on one review, the experience is also less than positive. Thus, it is *extremely* important that an editor treat everyone who submits to the journal with respect in terms of giving serious consideration to each paper, sending the paper out to persons who will give it a serious and constructive review, and ensuring that authors receive a fair and timely decision. In my view, journal editing is primarily about accepting the most significant manuscripts submitted and helping authors convey the importance of their work.

I have had papers rejected throughout my career—too many to count. When this happens, my perception of the journal depends on a few things. Was my paper reviewed by competent people who did a good job reviewing? Did they complete their reviews in a timely manner, and did the editor make a decision in a timely manner? These actions sound simple enough, but I will assert that they rarely happen together in the present day. Instead, most author stories are sad. Sad because the unprofessionalism that plagues our field and others is indeed a plague. It is common today to say "yes" to everything and then drop the ball on almost everything. Being late is now the rule rather than the exception. Excuses focus on simply being too busy rather than apologizing for not having the professional discipline to decline invitations when one's life is too complicated to be able to complete a constructive review in a timely manner.

When I agreed to serve as editor of EDPR in late 2005, I had only one goal: resuscitation. The journal, according to several people with whom I had spoken, was dead (similar to CEP back in 1990 when Ray Kulhavy took over). It had been several months since the last issue had been released and people just assumed there would be no more. Production was way behind and there was a struggle to fill issues. According to Ken Kiewra, the previous editor, the journal received around 30 submissions per year.

My editorial style was simple and straightforward. I tried to treat authors with respect by sending their manuscripts out for review within a day of receiving e-mail notification that a new submission had arrived. I tried to get good people to serve on the editorial board. In return for their service, I promised to not overburden them. This meant no more than 3–4 reviews per year. At the same time, I told board members that their term would be two years. After that, we would discuss whether they would continue to serve.

Not surprisingly, I had a few board members who, after immediately agreeing to serve on the board, rarely accepted an invitation to review. Others rarely completed their reviews on time. Some would submit a review that was barely a paragraph in length and reflected little effort. Fortunately, because EDPR used the Editorial Manager online system (as does CEP), I could see reviewer accountability data for each board member. When I would e-mail board members after the two-year period and ask if they wished to continue serving, the ones who e-mailed back within milliseconds and agreed to continue were the same members I had planned to discontinue. Some people are quite comfortable with the title of editorial board member but also quite uncomfortable with reviewing—or at least reviewing well and on time. The most difficult part of an editor's job is removing people from the board. But I have done so without hesitation. Others who either volunteered to serve as an ad hoc reviewer or were invited and subsequently did a good job were then invited to serve on the board.

When I became editor of EDPR, several people told me that I needed to get the "big names" on the masthead to give the journal credibility. If you look at the masthead today (Fred Paas retained most of my editorial board), I believe you will see fewer of these big names and more of the "up-and-comers." I can attest that oftentimes the big names are too busy to review (Rich Mayer is an exceptional exception here).

In 2006, my first year as editor of EDPR, we received 33 submissions. In 2015, my last year, we received 142. In 2006, the average number of days from when a manuscript is first received to the first decision was 51. In 2015, it was 26 days. With regard to Impact Factor, in 2008 it was 2.05. In 2016, it was 4.33.

I feel that I successfully resuscitated EDPR and kept it alive, and then oversaw it as it flourished. Moreover, I think EDPR has grown, and its reputation has improved. To use a direct quote from an article that appeared in CEP in 2012, "Among the five educational psychology journals sometimes considered the 'Big Five' (*Cognition and Instruction,* CEP, *Journal of Educational Psychology, Educational Psychologist,* and *Educational Psychology Review*) (Smith et al., 2003). *Educational Psychology Review* has the highest impact factor, at 3.477, the second highest impact factor of the 44 journals in the educational psychology category" (Mitchell & McConnell, 2012, p. 137).

As an editor, I was fortunate to lead EDPR to be recognized as the highest ranked Big Five journal.

Something I have always done as an editor is to personally e-mail reviewers to thank them for their reviews. I include the anonymized decision letter so they can see what other reviewers said. This is consistent with a developmental approach to reviewing and helps the younger reviewers by seeing other perspectives.

REFERENCES

Dobkin, D. (Director). (2004). *Wedding crashers* [Film]. Tapestry Films.

Hsieh, P.-H., Hsieh, Y.-P., Chung, W.-H., Acee, T., Thomas, G. D., Kim, H.-J., You, J., Levin, J. R., & Robinson, D. H. (2005). Is educational intervention research on the decline? *Journal of Educational Psychology, 97,* 523–529.

Mitchell, A. W., & McConnell, J. R. (2012). A historical review of *Contemporary Educational Psychology* from 1996 to 2010. *Contemporary Educational Psychology, 37,* 136–147.

Pattison, K. (2021). *Fossil men: The quest for the oldest skeleton and the origins of humankind.* William Morrow.

Robinson, D. H. (2004). An interview with Gene V Glass. *Educational Researcher, 33(3),* 26–30.

Robinson, D. H. (2011). Thoughts and recommendations concerning impact and productivity in school psychology journals. *Journal of School Psychology, 49,* 745–749.

Rowling, J. K. (199). *Harry Potter and the prisoner of Azkaban.* Scholastic.

Smith, M. C., Plant, M., Carney, R. N., Arnold, C. S., Jackson, A., Johnson, L. S., Lange Lange, H., Mathisa, F. S., & Smith, T. J. (2003). Productivity of educational psychologists in educational psychology journals, 1997–2001. *Contemporary Educational Psychology, 28,* 422–430.

FIGURES

Figure 1

My very First AERA in Boston. Here I am at the Bull & Finch Pub, Hoping to Run Into Norm and Cliff

Figure 2

My Second AERA, 1991 in Chicago. I Reunited With My Arizona State University Fellow Grad Students Sean Mulvenon (left) and John Behrens Who Was a New Assistant Professor at the University of Oklahoma

Figure 3

AERA in San Francisco, 1992. My Advisor, Ken Kiewra, and I Standing by My Poster. I was Likely Not Feeling Well. Also Notice My Tie. Yes, That's a Zipper Tie

Figure 4

1992 in San Francisco. One of the Few Times My Wife, Sheri, Accompanied Me

Figure 5

Our University of Nebraska Group Headed to the Annual Meeting of the Midwest Educational Research Association in October 1992. From Left, Rayne Sperling (Now at Penn State), Roger Bruning (Recently Retired after 50 years at Nebraska), the Late Christy Horn, Me, Joan Rankin, and Vicky Timme

Figure 6

August 2021. Ken Kiewra and I Remain Good Friends

ABOUT THE AUTHOR

Daniel H. Robinson is Associate Dean of Research in the College of Education at the University of Texas at Arlington. He received his PhD in Educational Psychology in 1993 from the University of Nebraska where he majored in both learning/cognition and statistics/research. He has taught at Mississippi State University (1993–1997), the University of South Dakota (1997–1998), the University of Louisville (1998–1999), the University of Texas at Austin (1999–2012), and Colorado State University (2012–2015). Dan has served as Editor of *Educational Psychology Review* from 2006–2015 and as Associate Editor of the *Journal of Educational Psychology* from 2014 to present. He has also served as an editorial board member of nine refereed international journals: *American Educational Research Journal, Contemporary Educational Psychology, Educational Technology, Research, & Development, Journal of Behavioral Education, Journal of Educational Psychology, Journal of Experimental Education, Reading Research and Instruction, Research in the Schools,* and *The Open Education Journal.*

Dan has published over 100 articles, books, and book chapters, presented over 100 papers at research conferences, and taught over 100 college courses. His research interests include educational technology innovations that may facilitate learning and team-based approaches to learning. He was a Visiting Fulbright Scholar, Victoria University, Wellington, New Zealand and was named as one of the most published authors in educational psychology journals from 1991–2002, 2003–2008, and 2009–2014, *Contemporary Educational Psychology,* 2004, 2010, 2015.

Lightning Source UK Ltd.
Milton Keynes UK
UKHW022147240522
403481UK00003B/66